Beauty Bar

Vegan Haircare Recipe Book

AuthorHouse™
1663 Liberty Drive
Bloomington, IN 47403
www.authorhouse.com
Phone: 833-262-8899

Because of the dynamic nature of the Internet, any web addresses or links contained in this book may have changed since publication and may no longer be valid. The views expressed in this work are solely those of the author and do not necessarily reflect the views of the publisher, and the publisher hereby disclaims any responsibility for them.

Any people depicted in stock imagery provided by Getty Images are models, and such images are being used for illustrative purposes only.
Certain stock imagery © Getty Images.

This book is printed on acid-free paper.

ISBN: 978-1-6655-1135-3 (sc)
ISBN: 978-1-6655-1136-0 (hc)
ISBN: 978-1-6655-1134-6 (e)

Library of Congress Control Number: 2020925003

Print information available on the last page.

Published by AuthorHouse 06/11/2021

authorHOUSE®

Dear Reader

I created this book to become a guide for natural
beauty seekers who love natural haircare

For questions, comments, promotion ads, email us at
kmorasvision@yahoo.com

Visit our website at
www.hair-boss-beauty-bar.myshopify.com
www.shop.saloninteractive.com/store/hairbossbeautybar

Services we provide
www.hairbossbeautybar.salonrunner.com

Design and Style

model snap kimorajada
ig kimoraa.jadaa
@adonis.bluebriads
stylist_kimberlysweets23
designer @yadiyda
makeup @toniacey
hair @trestylez404

Hair Boss
BEAUTY BAR

BIOTIN BOOST
Hair Serum

AMINO ACIDS
& HERBAL
EXTRACTS

Net Wt 1 oz.
(28 g)

Contents

Ginger For
Hair Growth

Ginger increases the scalp circulation that results in the flow of blood to the scalp. It also stimulates the hair follicles and encourages growth. The fatty acids in the ginger are beneficial for thin hair. ... Massage your scalp with it in circular motions and leave it about 30 minutes or longer.

Benefits of Vanilla Extract For Skin & Hair

Treatment of Acne

Properties of vanilla make it beneficial for the treatment of acne. Vanillin, though its antibacterial effects, helps cleanse your skin, reducing the occurrence of pimples and acne.

Anti-aging Benefits

Vanilla is rich in antioxidants which prevent and reverse skin damage caused by free radicals. It helps to slow down signs of ageing like fine lines, wrinkles and age spots. It is widely used in the cosmetic industry for its fragrance and anti-ageing benefits. Applying raw vanilla beans infused with organic oil imparts a great chocolaty fragrance besides making your skin smooth and soft.

Soothes Burns

Vanilla has been used as a traditional remedy to heal burns, wounds, and cuts concentrated vanilla extract or essential

Aloe Vera
For Hair

Aloe Vera is a plant that has thick leaves with a gel-like substance inside of them. ... Rubbing aloe vera into your scalp and hair and letting it peretrate your hair follicles could condition and improve damaged, dry hair. After letting it sit for an hour, rinse the gel off with a mild shampoo

Benefits for Hair Growth

Aloe vera contains something called proteolytic enzymes which repairs dead skin cells on the scalp. It also acts as a great conditioner and shiny. It promotes hair growth, prevent itching on the scalp, reduces dandruff and conditions your hair.

Aloe Vera
Pre-shampoo Treatment

Use aloe vera gel as a pre-shampoo treatment to reduce buildup dandruff. Aloe vera's natural enzymes destroy the excessive dead skin cells and fungus that leads to dandruff (malassezia) while also leaving the scalp's pH level balanced and hair moisturized. Apply to your scalp as a treatment before your wash and give yourself a fresh start! Massage the gel into your scalp and leave it for ten minutes, then rinse before shampooing or co-washing as usual.

You can also use aloe vera juice to the same end. For a lighter pre-shampoo treatment, mix aloe vera juice, cocount milk and wheat germ oil.

Cayenne Pepper
For Hair

Cayenne pepper contains capsaicin which is a compound that stimulates hair growth. The capsaicin stimulates blood circulation to the hair follicles, which ensures better nutrition and healthier hair growth. It also helps stimulate dormant hair follicles, and this helps increase hair volume and thickness

Olive Oil
Shampoo & Conditioner

Processing Time

1 hour

Process

1 - Chop the pepper into tiny pieces and to it add the olive oil.
2 - Pour the mixture into a jar and store it in a cool, dark place for 10 - 15 days.
3 - Ensure that the oil and discard the peppers.
4 - Strain the oil and discard the peppers.
5 - Take 2 - 3 tablespoons of the cayenne infused oil.
6 - Section your hair and apply this oil to your scalp and to the length of your hair until all of it is covered.
7 - Leave the oil in for an hour and then shampoo and condition.

How Often

You can repeat this up to twice a week.

Why This Works

The heat from the pepper improves the circulation of blood while the olive oil condition your hair.

Roasted Dark Whole Coffee Beans For Hair

Retention and absorption. Pour two cups of hair oil of your choice into a pan and add a quarter cup of roasted dark whole coffee beans the more the benefits they offer.

Cover the mixture and allow to cook in low heat for about eight hours ensuring you stir it at an interfal of every one hour so that it does not burn. Remove from the heat and strain the mixture.

Store the mixture in a cool, dark place. The oil can be used on the scalp, added to your shampoo or even added to the water of your final rinse.

Leave-in conditioner. After shampooing the hair, rinse it completely then gently squeeze excess water from hair. Pour brewed cool coffee into hair using a plastic container to catch the drippings. Continue pouring the coffee though the hair until all the drippings cease.

DIY Conditioner

If you'd rather go all natural, here's a very simple conditioning recipe:

1 - Cut the aloe vera leaf from the stem upward.
2 - Use a spoon to remove all the gel.
3 - Apply it to damp hair, starting at the scalp and working your way down to the ends.
4 - Wrap your hair in a warm, damp towel and let the treatment sink in for at least 15 minutes.
5 - Wash your hair as usual after the treatment.

Baking Soda & Honey Shampoo

"Shampoo" experience with baking soda and honey to clarify and moisturize hair is one such day of lovely preformance. My hair has been confused by the weather, too-frequent washing and lot of conditioners that I think built up to point of yuck. While I've done apple cider vinegar rinses before (I do about a 1/4 cup of cider vinegar in a mason jar

I've read that lots of people wash with baking soda frequently. For my hair, that tends to be dry and coarse/ curly, it will be a once-a-week event. If you do too much with the baking soda, it can dry your hair in a big way. But as a weekly fresh start, the honey & baking soda shampoo is genius for me.

In general, baking soda is abrasive and can leave your hair and scalp dry. Using the powder as a shampoo is more likely to be effective for people with extra oily hair. People with dry hair should consider following the rinse with a conditioner to moisturize the scalp.

There are a few simple ways to add some baking soda to shampoo regimen: sprinkle a bit of baking soda on your damp hair and then lather up. Add a bit of baking soda to the shampoo bar lather already in your hair, then add a bit more water and lather up.

Baking Soda & Honey Shampoo

Baking soda & honey
Mix Baking soda & honey
Stir well and apply

Repair Dry Hair with Apple Cider Vinegar

Use this shine-enhancing hair mask from **Tata Harper**, the founder of **" TATA HARPER SKINCARE ",** to repair dry and dull hair during the winter months. The **Apple Cider Vinegar** helps to remove product buildup that dulls hair and vitamin E-rich **Argan Oil** nourishes and softens unruly strands. Apple Cider Vinegar helps to **de-frizz hair**, according to **Natural Club**, making this a great choice for those with more texture.

Put the life back into your limp or damaged hair with this terrific home remedy:

combine 1 teaspoon Apple Cinder Vinegar with
2 tablespoons Olive Oil and
3 egg whites,
then rub the mix into your hair. Keep your hair...

Olive Oil And Cayenne Pepper

You will need

5-6 Cayenne Peppers
1 cup Olive Oil

Processing Time

1/2 hour

Process

Mix these 5-6 Cayenne Peppers and 1 cup Olive Oil, Allow it to settle for half an hour.

Rinse your hair with warm water. If you are short of time for this process, just add a few drops of raw honey into your conditioner and apply as you ordinarily would. Sit back and watch your hair blossom in no time.

Type

For those with dry damaged **hair, honey** comes in handy to boost the shine. It is a natural humectants that attracts moisture to the **hair**. It also has antioxidants and nutrients that nurture the **hair** follicles. Raw **honey** is the best as all the vitamins and other nutrients are preserved.

Why This Works

The heat from the pepper improves the circulation of blood while the olive oil conditions your hair.

1 -Chop the pepper into tiny pieces and to it add the olie oil.
2 -Pour the mixture into a jar and store it in a cool, dark place for 10 - 15 days.
3 -Ensure that the oil is stored away from sunlight.
4 -Strain the oil and discard the peppers.
5 -Take 2 - 3 tablespoons of the cayenne infused oil.
6 -Section your hair and apply this oil to your scalp and to the length of your hair until all of it is covered.
7 -Leave the oil in for an hour and then shampoo and condition.

Honey

Honey has both emollient and humectant properties, making it a great hair moisturizer. Emollients smooth the hair follicles, adding shine to dull hair. Humectants bond with water molecules, adding moisturizing and locking in shine, honey can help restore the natural luster of your hair.

Honey is a good treatment for those who suffer from hair loss. Mixing raw honey with cinnamon and olive oil will make for a great treatment for hair loss. Other than offering the growth, honey will also soften your hair.

Reverse Sun Damage
With Honey

Whatever your hair-gehydrating demon is - hard water, sun overexposure, or your trusty flat iron - nature's sweetener can help. " Honey " is a natural humectant, which means it attracts and locks in moisture, " Cox says. While this honey mask may seem like a bit of a sticky situation, it works well on all hair types.

To use: Massage approximately 1/2 cup honey into clean, damp hair, let sit for 20 minutes, then rinse with warm water. You can also add 1 to 2 Tbsp olive oil to loosen the honey for easier application. For extremely sun-damaged hair, trying mixing honey with 1 to 2 Tbsp of a protein- rich ingredient, like avocado or egg yolk, which will help replenish the keratin protein bonds that UV rays attack. Treatment can be applied once a month.

Strengthen Fragile Hair with Ginger

Why Ginger is such a Good Hair Care Ingredient

Does your hair feel weak and fragile? Does it

Because of ginger's restorative powers—as well as its age-old reputation for restoring strength and vitality—it's a natural fit for the **Whole Blends Ginger Recovery collection.**

These formulas infused with ginger and golden honey, were created to help strengthen the most exhausted.

Now, for the honey. The idea is that honey is a humectant- it is great for creating and maintaining moisture. While some people follow up the baking soda step with the Apple Cider Vinegar rinse I described above (If you have fine hair, oily hair or super-product- loaded hair, I would try that) I needed more of a conditioner. The idea is that the honey mix stays on your hair, so this one requires a really diluted solution of honey in water. I used a tablespoon of honey in 4 cups of very warm water. Stir, stir, stir! You do not want a glop of honey in one part of your hair and none in another.

Mix 1/4 cup of raw honey with water. Ensure it gets thin enough to spread on your hair. Add it to your hair using tablespoon measurements. Apply it to damp hair the way you would ordinarily apply shampoo. Spread it event across your entire head.

Ginger

Ginger offers head-to-toe benefits, and when incorporated into hair care formulas, like a routine that includes shampoo with ginger, the bundle can help restore to bouncy, shiny health. Here everything you need to know about ginger and what makes it such good ingredient in hair products.

Does your hair feel week and fragile? Does it look a little lifeless?

You might want to try a product with ginger for hair. While the spice may be a regular ingredient in your kitchen, it's less common in your beauty routine. That's about to change.

Hair loss treatment. No woman likes to lose their hair as this even affects their self-confidence.

Caffeine in coffee is great for hair. When a topical application is done on the hair or scalp, it finds its way to the roots and stimulates them. Improving its structure and growth. Caffeine can thus restore hair growth and/ or prevent hair loss.

Manageable hair

Coffee brew can be used to detangle the hair. It makes the hair shaft stronger and smoother making it easier to manage while.

Oil

Coffee oil blood circulation in the scalp and stimulates the roots of the hair. The phytosterois in the oil promotes moisture retention and absorption. Pour two cups of hair oil of your choice into a pan and add a quarter cup of roasted dark whole coffee beans. The darker the beans the more benefits they offer.

Moisturize Dull Hair With Dairy

Anything from harsh styling products and air pollution can sap moisture and dull shine - but dairy products like sour cream and plain yogurt can help to reverse this damage. " Lactic Acid gently strips away dirt while the milk fat moisturizes, " says Lisa Belkin, author of The Cosmetics Cookbook. While this mask can work for all hair types, the protein in the yogurt is especially great for enhancing natural curis.

To use

Massage 1/'2 cup sour cream or plain yogurt into damp hair and let sit for 20 minutes. Rinse with warm water, followed by cool water, then, shampoo hair as you normally would. Treatment can be applied every other week.

Heighten Your Shine
With Tea

Some of us need tea to get the day started and bring us back to life, and as it just so happens, it can have the same effect on your hair. If you've noticed your hair has been looking a bit dull lately, black tea is a great way to add a revitalized shine to your locks, according to Lifealth. If you're already a tea drinker the thi-at- home remedy is going to be super simple to add in to your routine. And even if you're not. it's still pretty darn easy. Bonus: Black tea has also been known to help with curl loss.

To use

Brew some black tea and let it sit until it's............

Revitalize Your Hair With Bananas

It's no secret that bananas are good for us - they're nutrient packed and high in potassium, which helps regulate our bodies. And all of those great benefits help make bananas an amazing choice for hair mask. According to Healthline, bananas **contain the mineral silica**, which helps your body to synthesize collagen, which can make your body to synthesize collagen, which can make your hair stronger and thicker. A banana hair mask can also reportedly moisturize your hair and help relieve a dry, itchy scalp.

To use

Blend together two ripe bananas and halt a cup of coconut milk. Coat your hair in the mixture and let it sit for 30 minutes, then wash the mask out of your hair.

Covered for about a half hour using plastic wrap or a shower cap, then shampoo and rinse.

Bring The Bounce With Beer

To add body to hair, reach for an unlikely beauty beverage: beer! The **fermented drink** contains generous supplies of yeast and B vitamins, which works to plump tired strands, Cox explains.

To use

Mix 1/2 sup flat beer (pour beer into a container and let it sit out for a couple of hours to deplete carbonation) with 1 tsp light oil

(sunflower or canola) and raw egg. Apply to clean, damp hair, let sit for 15 minutes, then rinse with cool water. Or add flat beer only to a spray bottle and spritz onto dry hair. " When the liquid evaporates, the remaining protein residue (from the wheat malt or hops) continues to strengthen and structure hair, " Belkin says. Treatments can be appied every other week.

(If your hair's oily, skip your scalp) clip hair in place and let sit for 15 minutes, then rinse and cleaned with shampoo. Do this at least once a month.

Transform All Hair Types With Eggs

"The [raw] **egg** is really the best of all words, " says **Janice Cox**, author of ***Natural Beauty at Home***. The yolk, rich in fats and proteins, is naturally moisturizing, while the white, which contains bacteria-eating enzymes, removes unwanted oils, she explains.

To use

For normal hair, use the entire egg to condition hair; use egg whites only to treat oily hair; use egg

yolks only to moisturize dry, brittle hair, Cox says. Blend about 1/2 cup of which ever egg mixture is appropriate for you and apply to clean, damp hair. If there isn't enough egg to coat scalp and hair, use more as needed. Leave on for 20 mintues, rinse with cool water (to prevent egg from " cooking ") and shampoo hair. Whole egg and yolks- condition hair; use egg whites only treatments can be applied once a month, while whites-only treatment can be applied every two weeks, Cox says.

Guava Leaves And Fruits
With Hair

These are rich in vitamin C which is known to prevent hair fall. These fruits boost your collagen production and the good thing is that you can use the leaves to make your own hair growth solution.

You're basically getting more than one benefit from Guavas!

Relieve An Itchy Scalp
With Lemon

To fight winter dryness, try a lemon juice and olive oil mixture in your hair. " The acidity in lemon juice helps rid your scalp of any loose, dry flakes of skin, while the olive oil moisturizes the [newly exposed] skin on your head, " Cox says.

To use

Mix
2 Tbsp fresh lemon juice
2 Tbsp olive oil
2 Tbsp water
And massage into damp scalp. Let mixture sit for 20 mintues, then rinse and shampoo hair.

Treatment can be applied every other week

How to use Rice Water for Hair /
How to make Rice Water

Rice water: the milky liquid leftover when you soak rice for several hours.

1 -It promotes hair growth
2 -It contains: Antioxidants,Vitamin B6,E, Amino acids, Organic acids, and inositol
   a sugar molecule, that may protect hair from breakage.
3 -Softening, detangles , strengthening,, makes hair shinier, supports hair growth.
4 -Moisturizer for skin, reduce eczema, decrease dermatitis, increase circulation
   of skin .

How to make rice water:

1 cup rice : organic rice, white , or whole grain
1 cup water : use filtered if you can

Add rice and water , let it sit for several hours , strain the rice ,let the rice water sit in a glass container for 12- 24 hours, then freeze or refrigerate water until use , add essential oil of your desire, only a few drops. This will add a more pleasant smell , to the water .

Use directly on your hair and face ,after shampooing, or use as a pro poo . Before shampoo let it sit for 20 minutes or use as a protein treatment, after you shampoo your hair let it sit for 20 minutes then rinse well.

Use this once or twice a month, careful of usage.

Use on clean skin for face moisturizer to soften skin.

If you have a none rice allergy, do not use.

hair-boss-beauty-bar.mydhopify.com

Printed in the United States
by Baker & Taylor Publisher Services